# Persevering Beyond Sexual Harassment

# Volume 2

# My Journal

# Preface

In Volume1, we share many facts, statistics, resources, and personal experiences with our readers regarding Sexual Harassment. We would like to provide a *journal* for the readers as well who have been violated or affected by this. It can be a huge support to build back the self motivation and esteem just by recording your experiences. Communicating about the experience even on paper; can provide a healing trend to your soul and close some wounds which scarred your heart. This seventeen-day journal will build you back into a woman of character and will break the silence over the past occurrences. You are a winner and champion over this!

# Quiz or Recap

1.What does sexual harassment mean to you?_____

_____

_____

_____

_____

_____

2. Who can experience sexual harassment?

_____

_____

3. Does sexual harassment make one bitter?

_____

_____

4. Are there agencies and laws to prohibit and protect those whom have been violated?

_____

_____

5. Who do you report sexual harassment to in the workplace?

_____

_____

in the church

_____

# Day One

## Encourage yourself by building Self value

# Day Two

## Getting past the offense

# Day Three

## Getting Past the Offender

# Day Four

## Reporting your offense

# Day Five

# Record
# (write it down)

# Day Six

How did you feel after the first incident?

# Day Seven

## Did you tell anyone?

# Day Eight

Were you afraid or embarrassed?

# Day Nine

## Did they believe you?

# Day Ten

Did you co workers or peers treat you in different?

# Day Eleven

In the process of the investigation, if there was an investigation; how did you empower yourself? What measures did you take in order to remain focus?

# Day Twelve

# Were you afraid of the results before it was given?

# Day Thirteen

## What are were results? Record them

# Day Fourteen

Were you astounded at the results?

# Day Fifteen

Were you satisfied and are you still angry with the offender?

# Day Sixteen

## What steps are you taking to empower other women?

# Day Seventeen

Now you are an over comer!

## More Books and Resources

### Kids Corner
*Kid's activity Book*
*Making Cents*
*Coping with Autism*

### Entrepreneurial resources
*Women 2 Women*
*The Entrepreneurs Handbook & Guide*
*The National Extraordinary Professional Women Handbook*
*The National Extraordinary Professional Women Magazine*

*Women! What's in your Purse?*
*Women! IS coffee good for business?*
*Winning the War of Anxiety*

### Christian Literature
*Becoming an effective leader in ministry Volumes I, II, & III.*
*Breaking Generational Patterns*
*Seven Steps to a fall of A Clergy*
*The Fruits of the Spirit*
*The Professional Pastors Magazine*
*In the shoes of A Prophet (the role of a Prophet)*

- All books can be found on Amazon.com, Kindle Fire, and some Barnes & Noble.

# About the Author

Diane is the senior pastor of Saint Petersburg Global Ministries, and Chief Empowerment coach/officer of the National Extraordinary Professional Women. Her hobbies are reading the infallible written Word of God; golf and tennis. There are additional non profits in which she manages for a better future of individuals.

Her organizations have online broadcasts to effective train, educate, and empower men and women globally.

www.ingramcontent.com/pod-product-compliance
Lightning Source LLC
Chambersburg PA
CBHW041142180526
45159CB00002BB/702